ANNO'S AESOP

A BOOK OF FABLES BY AESOP AND MR. FOX • RETOLD AND ILLUSTRATED BY

MITSUMASA ANNO

REINHARDT BOOKS

IN ASSOCIATION WITH

VIKING

Contents

MR. FOX'S FABLES
Foreword

One day, at the edge of the forest, little Freddy Fox found something. He had never seen anything like it before. Perhaps someone had forgotten it, he thought. But it was rather dirty, so maybe it had fallen off the garbage truck. What could it be? Freddy picked it up and hurried home to show it to his father. "That's what is called a book, Freddy," said his father. "Books are full of wonderful stories. People like to read them." "Oh, *please* read this book to me!" Freddy begged his

Mr. Fox's Fables

Notes

father. But his father only said, "I'm too sleepy now. I'll read it to you tomorrow." Maybe Mr. Fox was just making excuses. Maybe he couldn't read at all. But Freddy would not give up. He begged and begged for a story, so finally his father began to read out loud to him. Some of the stories in this book are what Mr. Fox read to Freddy. Or was he just pretending to read? That's Mr. Fox's secret! Let's listen to his stories.

The Fox and the Grapes

A hungry fox saw some fine bunches of grapes hanging from a vine that grew along a high trellis. He did his best to reach them by jumping as high as he could, but it was all in vain, for they were just out of reach. Soon he gave up trying and walked away with an air of dignity and unconcern, saying, "I really didn't want those grapes, anyhow. I thought they were ripe but now I see that they are quite sour."

It's easy to despise what you cannot get.

This story is a little bit sad, Freddy (said Mr. Fox). Once there was a musician named Scaramouche who loved a pretty girl. He came to her house and sang:

Look out the window, my pretty dove,
And I will sing you a song of my love.

However, the pretty girl in the house didn't love him at all. She wouldn't even go to the window. Instead, she told her grandmother to stick a funny wooden puppet's head out the window and tell Scara to go away.

Poor Scara was terribly disappointed, but he didn't want to admit it. So he sang another song:

> *Forget my love ditty; ignore what I said;*
> *I see you're not pretty, but ugly instead.*

But that fox over there was not fooled by Scara's new song. "Don't pretend not to care about something when you really do," he told Scara. "That's just 'sour grapes.'"

The Bear and the Travelers

Two travelers were on the road together, when a bear suddenly appeared. Before the bear saw them, one man made for a tree at the side of the road, and climbed up into the branches and hid there. The other was not so nimble as his companion. Since he could not escape, he threw himself on the ground and pretended to be dead. The bear came up and sniffed all around him, but he kept perfectly still and held his breath, for they say that a bear will not touch a dead body. The bear was fooled and thought he was a corpse, and finally went away.

Two men were taking a nap under an oak tree when suddenly some bears came by. One man heard them—he woke up and hastily climbed into the tree for safety. Then one of the bears walked up to the sleeping man and began to lick his ear hungrily. It surely would have eaten him, but the man in the tree threw acorns at all the bears until finally they gave up and went away. Having saved his friend's life, he then came down from the tree and spoke to the man on the ground. "Weren't you scared when that bear licked your ear?" he asked.

When the coast was clear, the traveler in the tree came down, and asked the other what it was the bear had whispered to him when he put his mouth to his ear. The other replied, "He told me never again to travel with a friend who deserts at the first sign of danger!"

Misfortune tests the sincerity of friendship.

"*Bear! What* bear? You must have been dreaming!" exclaimed the one who had been asleep. "And why did you throw all these acorns at me?"

There also seems to be an arithmetic problem here. It asks, "How many bears are there? How many men are there? How many are there all together?" But can you add bears and men together? That's a hard question. It's all right, though, I guess. After all, it's not like adding up acorns and men together, is it? Can you see why?

The Dog and His Reflection

A dog was crossing a plank bridge over a stream with a piece of meat in his mouth, when he happened to see his own reflection in the water. He thought it was another dog with a piece of meat, so he let go of his own and flew at the other dog to get his piece, too. But, of course, all that happened was that he got neither, for one was only a reflection and the other was carried away by the stream.

Envy not your neighbor's lot;
be content with what you've got.

1

Once upon a time there was a dog, so the story goes (said Mr. Fox). It was a stray dog, so it wasn't wearing a collar. Since they aren't tied up, stray dogs can go wherever they please, but no one feeds them. They have to find their own meals. This dog had found a nice steak for himself. The fisherman in the boat had brought it for his lunch, but the dog stole it. Just then, along came another dog with another steak. "Let's have a picnic," he proposed. "Yes, let's," agreed the first dog. But then,

along came two other dogs who had nothing to eat. Would the first two dogs have to share their food with the newcomers? No, Freddy, I've got it wrong. These aren't *new* dogs. They're the same two dogs, but they've eaten their steaks now. How confusing! Perhaps this is really another arithmetic problem. Four dogs divided by two is two dogs. Two steaks divided by two dogs is . . . ?

morning the turtle decided to surprise the rabbit by visiting *his* side of the ditch. He got up very early, while the rabbit was still asleep, crawled to the edge of the ditch and gave a great big leap. But it was the turtle who got the surprise, for he was not a good jumper at all, and he slid right down to the bottom of the ditch! It took him all day to clamber out!

The Rabbit and the Turtle

One day a rabbit was making fun of a turtle for being so slow. "Wait a bit," said the turtle. "I'll run a race with you and I'll bet that I win." "Oh, well," replied the rabbit, who was much amused by the idea, "let's try and see." They agreed that the fox should set a course for them and be the judge. When the time came, both started out together, but the rabbit was soon so far ahead that he thought he might as well have a little rest. Down he lay and fell fast asleep. Meanwhile the turtle kept plodding on and finally reached the goal. At last the rabbit woke up with a start, and dashed on as fast as he could, only to find that the turtle had already won the race.

Slow and steady wins the race.

Wait a minute! This picture is upside down. See, if you turn the book around you can tell what's going on. It's a story about a turtle and a rabbit. They were the best of friends, although they lived on opposite sides of a very deep ditch. Whenever they wanted to play together they always met on the turtle's side of the ditch. The rabbit, who was a very good jumper, would just jump across. But one

The Donkey
in the Lion's Skin

A donkey found a lion's skin and dressed himself up in it. Then he went about frightening everyone he met, for they all took him to be a lion, men and beasts alike, and ran away when they saw him coming. Elated by the success of his trick, he opened his mouth and brayed loudly. The fox heard him and recognized him at once for the donkey. He said to the donkey, "Oho, my stupid friend, it's you, isn't it! I'd have been afraid of you too if I hadn't heard your loud voice!"

A strong voice often reveals a weak mind.

"Let's put on a play," said the fox one day. "I'll be the director, and tell you all what to do." "Why do *you* always have to be the boss?" objected the dog. "Because I'm the cleverest. We foxes are all clever," replied the fox. "Now, donkey, here's a lion's skin for you. You be a lion," he ordered. So the donkey slipped into the lion's skin and said timidly, "A-a-rgh! A-a-rgh! Aren't you afraid of me?" "Oh, that's

terrible," said the fox. "Why can't you be more fierce?" "It's not fair!," barked the dog. "I'd be a much better lion than that stupid donkey!" And with that, the dog yanked the lion's skin off the donkey. "No! Stop!" shouted the fox. "Oh, look, you've gone and torn it up. If you want to be the lion in our play you'll have to get us another lion's skin. Go to the old lion and see if he'll trade you a real lion's skin for this one."

continued on page 14

The Old Lion

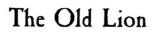

A lion, enfeebled by age and no longer able to get food for himself by force, decided to do so by cunning instead. He lay down inside a cave and pretended to be ill. Whenever any of the other animals came into the cave to inquire how he felt, he sprang upon them and devoured them. Many lost their lives in this way until, one day, a fox called at the cave, and, having a suspicion of the truth, spoke to the lion from the outside

(continued on page 16)

A few days later, the fox went to visit the old lion. He found the lion in a very grouchy mood. "What's the matter?" asked the fox. The lion growled and replied, "Just yesterday the dog came and told me to trade my skin for an old torn one that he had. That made me angry, of course. *'And were you planning to kill me to get my skin?'* I roared at him. And what do you think he replied? He said that those were *your* orders! So now what do you have to say for yourself?" The lion was in a rage. The fox replied, "Oh,

The Fox and the Goat

A fox fell into a well and couldn't get out again. By and by a thirsty goat came by and, seeing the fox in the well, asked him if the water was good. "Good?" said the fox. "It's the best water I ever tasted in all my life. Come down and try it yourself." The goat thought of nothing but how thirsty he was, and jumped right in. When he had had enough to drink, he looked about for some way to get out, but of course there was none. Then the fox said, "I have a good idea. You stand on your hind legs and

(continued on page 17)

that was just a joke. I really sent the dog here hoping you would scold him for having torn up the valuable skin of a lion." Now wasn't that a clever lie, Freddy? We foxes certainly know how to fool people. We're clever. What makes some of us so clever is the water in this well. It's a kind of magic medicine. The fox you see here was just taking a drink when the goat came along and asked, "May I have some of that water, too?" I don't think it's going to work for the goat, though. Goats are not very bright.

continued on page 16

(continued from page 14)

rather than going in. "How are you?" he asked the lion. The lion replied that he was very ill indeed. "But," said he, "why do you stand outside? Do come in." "I would have done so," answered the fox, "if I hadn't noticed that all the footprints point toward the cave and none the other way."

Foresight is better than hindsight.

I'd never drink any medicine of that kind, anyway. I don't need to. And you'd better not either, Freddy. But the story goes on like this. The silly goat went down into the well to take a drink of the "magic water." Then, of course, he couldn't get out. Too bad! He really did want to become clever like us. Meanwhile, the fox went back to see the lion again. "I'm sorry I made you angry," he said. "Let me make up for it by building you a nice castle." And it says here that he made the lion a (continued from page 15) plant your forelegs firmly against the side of the well. Then I'll climb onto your back and, from there, by stepping on your horns, I can get out. And when I'm out, I'll help you out, too." The goat did as he was asked, and the fox climbed onto his back and so out of the well. Then he coolly walked away. The goat called loudly after him and reminded him of his promise to help him out, but the fox merely turned and said, "If you had as much sense in your head as you have hairs in your beard you wouldn't have jumped into the well without making sure that you could get out again."

Look before you leap.

grand castle surrounded by wooden bars, and around it he dug a deep moat. "Now you'd be safe even if a *hundred* dogs came to attack you," he declared. The lion was delighted. He thanked the fox, saying that at last he'd be able to sleep in peace, knowing that no one would be able to attack him. Would you want a castle like that? Yes? But just think—if you lived in a castle like that, your enemies wouldn't be able to come in, but you wouldn't be able to get out, either!

The Donkey
and His Burdens

A peddler who owned a donkey one day bought a large quantity of salt and loaded up his poor beast with as much as he could carry. On the way home the donkey stumbled as he was crossing a stream and fell into the water. The salt got thoroughly wet and much of it melted and drained away, so that, when he got on his legs again, the donkey found that his load had become much lighter. His master, however, drove him back to town and bought

This is a story about a donkey that had been tied to a pear tree with a heavy load of wheat on his back. Another donkey who happened to pass by had asked him why he was tied to the tree. "I don't know," said the first donkey. "I've never done anything wrong." "Well, if that is the case," said the second donkey, "I'll just untie that rope for you." Actually, Freddy, this donkey had never been tied up when he was little. I think it was only after he had grown big enough to carry heavy loads that he had been tied to a tree. Maybe that's

more salt, which he added to what remained in the baskets, and started out again. No sooner had they reached a stream than the donkey lay down in it and rose, as before, with a much lighter load. But his master detected the trick, and turning back once more, bought a large number of sponges and piled them on the donkey's back. When they came to the stream the donkey again lay down. But this time, as the sponges soaked up the water, he found when he got up on his legs again that he had a bigger burden to carry than ever.

You may use a good trick once too often.

because his owner thought, "This donkey isn't worth much, but I don't want it to run away with my wheat on its back." Anyway, the donkey was set free. He hadn't been free in a long time, so he ran around happily without looking where he was going, and—*oops!* He landed in the river! The man who was supposed to be minding him saw him and cried, "Oh, no! The wheat's all wet and the donkey's about to drown! My master's going to be angry. What shall I do?"

The Goat and the Donkey

A goat was jealous of a donkey because their master fed the hardworking donkey well but made the goat find his own food in the field. One day the goat said to the donkey, "If you will follow my advice, I'll tell you how to stop working so hard. Just pretend you have gone crazy and jump over the cliff and you will be able to have a good rest." The donkey did as he suggested, and of course he broke his legs and was badly hurt. His owner sent for the animal doctor and asked him how to cure his donkey. "Just boil that goat's lungs and give the broth to the donkey and he will be fine," advised the doctor. So the goat was killed and the donkey was cured.

When you plot to do harm to others, it is you who will be hurt.

Well, here is the rest of the story. They got the donkey out of the water, but he had lost the wheat and broken his leg. The animal doctor bandaged it and put a splint on it. It says here, "The donkey's keeper was scolded for not keeping the donkey tied up." But one of these goats seems to know what really happened, and he's scolding the other donkey in the middle. He's saying "It's *your* fault for untying his rope. That's why the poor donkey broke his leg. You should apologize for causing all

this trouble." It says that the donkey asked the goat, "So which one do you want me to apologize to? That man? Or the donkey?" But the goat couldn't tell him. Goats are not at all clever, you remember. Hm-m. There's another donkey up on the edge of the cliff. Doesn't he know it's dangerous up there? Wait a minute. It says here, "This isn't *another* donkey. It's the donkey that broke its leg." I see, it's just in the wrong order.

The Bald Man and the Fly

A fly settled on the head of a bald man and bit him. In his eagerness to kill it, the man hit himself a smart slap. But he missed the fly, who said to him in derision, "You tried to kill me for just one little bite—what will you do to yourself now for the heavy smack you have just given yourself?" "Oh, for that blow I bear no grudge," replied the bald man, "for I never intended myself any harm. But as for you, you contemptible insect who live by sucking human blood, I'd have borne a good deal more for the satisfaction of dashing the life out of you!"

A mistake need not be punished, but even a tiny evil should be wiped out.

Now here's a new story. Somebody was stealing a farmer's ripe wheat. The farmer needed this wheat to feed his chickens, so he was very upset. He decided to hide in the flower bed and watch to see who the thief might be. Peeking out, he saw a grasshopper flying away, and he shouted, "Stop, thief! I know you're the one who's been stealing my wheat!" "Oh, no," said the grasshopper. "I was down in my home underground when your wheat ripened. I've never even *seen* any ripe wheat." If

The Ants

Ants were once human beings, and made their living by tilling the soil. But, not content with the results of their own work, they were always casting longing eyes upon the crops and fruits of their neighbors, which they stole whenever they got the chance. At last their covetousness made Jupiter so angry that he changed them into ants. But, though their forms were changed, their natures remained the same. And so, to this day, they go about the fields and gather the fruits of others' labor and store them up for their own use.

You may punish a thief, but his bad character remains.

you can say you weren't there when something happened, Freddy (said Mr. Fox), that means you have what's called an *alibi*. The grasshopper had a good alibi. This is sort of like a mystery story, and the fun of it is trying to find out who the real thief is. Actually, there's something suspicious going on underground. But the farmer can't see what's happening down there. So who really stole the wheat? Can you figure it out, Freddy? Let me give you a hint: it is definitely not the mole!

The Farmer and the Fox

A farmer was greatly annoyed by a fox, who came prowling about his yard at night and carried off his chickens. So he set a trap for him and caught him. In order to be revenged upon him, he tied a bunch of straw to his tail and set fire to it and let him go. As ill luck would have it, however, the fox made straight for the fields where the wheat was standing ripe and ready for harvesting. It quickly caught fire and was all burned up, and the farmer lost his whole crop.

Revenge is a two-edged sword.

Now maybe they'll catch the thief. But the farmer's fields are burning! It looks as if the thief who stole the chickens' wheat may have set the fields on fire to destroy any evidence. That's what you might think. But we figured out that it must have been the ants who stole the wheat, didn't we? And ants don't use fire, do they? So it must have been the farmer himself. Probably he set fire to the ants' nest to force them out, and the wheat also caught fire. The lesson here is: Don't lose all of your wheat by begrudging someone a small part of it.

The Fox and the Crow

A crow was sitting on a branch of a tree with a piece of cheese in her beak when a fox noticed her and set his wits to work to find some way of getting the cheese for himself. Coming and standing under the tree, he looked up and said, "What a noble bird I see above me! Her beauty is without equal; the hue of her plumage is exquisite. If only her voice is as sweet as her looks are fair, she surely ought to be the queen of the birds." The crow was hugely flattered by this, and just to show the fox that she could sing she gave a loud caw. Down came the cheese, of course, and the fox, snatching it up, said, "You have a voice, ma'am, but what you lack is brains."

Beware of flatterers.

This is a different story. It's called "The Fox's Advice." The fox is calling to the crow on the tree, "Hey, you up there! Are you trying to eat the moon? How greedy you are! But if you really want to eat the whole moon, you should wait another two weeks. Then it will be twice as big as it is now. Surely you can wait until then, can't you?" But the crow doesn't reply. He can't say a word. Why not? Because his beak is full. He's holding the moon there and so he can't open his beak.

The Grasshopper
and the Ants

One fine day in winter some ants were busy drying their store of grain, which had gotten rather damp during a long spell of rain. Presently, up came a grasshopper and begged them to spare her a few kernels of wheat. "For," she said, "I'm simply starving." The ants stopped work for a moment, though this was against their principles. "May we ask," said they, "what you were doing with yourself all last summer? Why didn't you collect a store

It's cold outside, and snow is on the ground. People have to play indoors, where it is warm. But look, someone has come walking across the snow. This must be the farmer from the story before. He has been traveling all over, disguised as a musician, in search of the thief who stole his wheat. And now winter has come. It is too cold for him, and he doesn't have any food, but he sees a house ahead and he walks toward it. He can hear people dancing and talking inside. I hope they will let him

of food for the winter?" "The fact is," replied the grasshopper, "I was so busy singing that I hadn't the time." "If you spent the summer singing," replied the ants, "then you will have to spend the winter dancing." And they chuckled and went on with their work.

In times of plenty, set aside something
for a time of need.

come in. But what is the grasshopper doing, you ask? Well, Freddy, it looks as if he is running away. But yes, as you say, the grasshopper has an alibi, so he doesn't really need to run away. You're absolutely right. I had forgotten to read what it says here. It says, "The grasshopper isn't running away. He just stopped by to warn the ants that they should watch out for the farmer, who has come looking for them." Insects look after one another, you see.

These birds are called alligator birds. They eat what gets stuck between
the alligator's teeth. This keeps the teeth clean and at the same time the
birds get enough to eat. It's a very good arrangement for all of them.
But one day along came a wily crane who was planning to play a mean
trick on the wolf. He showed the wolf what good friends the alligator
and the alligator birds were. Then he said, "My dear friend, I'm a den-
tist. Let me clean your teeth the way those alligator birds are cleaning

The Wolf and the Crane

A wolf once got a bone stuck in his throat. So he went to a crane and begged her to put her long bill down his throat and pull it out. "I'll reward you well," he promised. The crane did as she was asked, and got the bone out quite easily. The wolf thanked her warmly and was just turning away when she cried, "What about that reward of mine?" "Well, what about it?" snapped the wolf, baring his teeth as he spoke. "You can go around boasting that you once put your head into a wolf's mouth and didn't get it bitten off. What more do you want?" So the wolf got what he wanted and the crane was cheated of her reward.

The weak cannot demand justice from the strong.

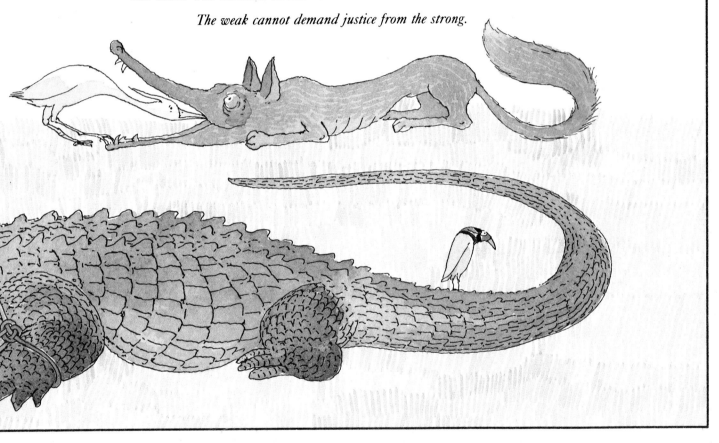

the alligator's teeth." You see, the crane had always had a grudge against the wolf. Now the crane planned to fool the wolf into thinking he was a nice, helpful friend. Then, when the wolf opened his mouth, the wicked crane was going to poke the soft part of his throat with his sharp beak. *Ouch!* Well, the wolf pretended to believe the crane. But do you think he was fooled? Not at all. He was just waiting for his dinner to come right into his mouth by itself!

The Fox
and the Stork

A fox invited a stork to dinner, at which the only food he provided was a large flat dish of soup. The fox lapped it up with great pleasure, but the stork with her long bill tried in vain to drink a drop of the delicious broth. Her evident distress made the sly fox laugh. But not long after this the stork invited the fox in turn, and set before him a pitcher with a long,

Now this is a story about a charming fox and a rude stork who were neighbors. One day the fox invited the stork to lunch. He served fish, because it was the stork's favorite dish. The stork ate greedily, using her beak like pincers. But the fox, poor fellow, could hardly eat at all, as he was afraid of getting a bone stuck in his throat. However, he was too polite to mention it to his guest. The next day, the stork invited the fox to lunch at her house, although to say that she was returning the fox's

narrow neck, into which she could get her bill with ease. Now it was the stork's turn to laugh, for, while she enjoyed her dinner, the fox sat by, hungry and helpless, as it was impossible for him to reach the tempting contents of the pitcher.

He who laughs last laughs best.

favor may be too much of an exaggeration. She served honey and milk in two tall jars. Can you see how polite the fox was? He took small mouthfuls one at a time by tipping his jar a little bit. But this stork! She has stuck her head right inside the jar! What bad manners! Besides, she has left herself defenseless. A fox would never do such a thing. A fox would never be caught off guard.

The Boy Who Cried Wolf

A shepherd boy was tending his flock near a village and thought it would be great fun to fool the villagers by pretending that a wolf was attacking the sheep. He shouted out, "Wolf! Wolf!" and when the people came running up he laughed at them for their pains. He did this more than once, and each time the villagers found they had been tricked, for there was no wolf at all. At last, one day a wolf really did come, and again the boy cried, "Wolf! Wolf!" as loudly as he could. But the people were so used to hearing

(continued on page 34)

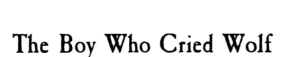

Once there was a little shepherd boy named Peter. The villagers thought he had stolen a chicken. They were terribly angry and ran after him to punish him. Usually, Freddy, when a chicken is stolen, it is a fox or a weasel or even a dog or a snake that has done it, but

perhaps children sometimes do, too. Anyway, that is what the village people thought. They were very superstitious people, and they had the idea that Peter was really a fox who had changed himself into the shape of a boy.

(continued from page 32)

him call that they paid no attention to his cries for help. And so the wolf had it all his own way, and killed off sheep after sheep at his leisure.

You cannot believe a liar even when he is telling the truth.

The Farmer and His Sons

A certain farmer had several sons who were always quarreling with one another, and, try as he might, he could not get them to live together in harmony. So he made up his mind to convince them of their foolishness by the following means: First, he asked them to fetch a bundle of sticks, and challenged each in turn to break it across his knee. All tried and all failed. Then he undid the bundle and handed them the sticks one by one. This time they had no trouble at all in breaking them. "There, my sons," said he. "You can see that when you are united you will be more than a match for your enemies, but if you quarrel and separate, your weakness will put you at the mercy of those who would attack you."

Union is strength.

This is still the same story. When the villagers actually counted their chickens, they found that not a single one was missing. They realized that they had made a mistake in thinking Peter had stolen a chicken. "We must apologize to that innocent boy," they said. "Let's have a party for him to show him that we're sorry." But look! The sheep are running! Peter is running, too! "Wolf! Wolf!" he was shouting. "A wolf is after

the sheep!" But the villagers didn't hear Peter. They were having such a good time that they didn't notice what was going on outside the walls. So the hungry wolf caught all the sheep it wanted for its dinner. And Peter never got to the party that was given for him. The foolish villagers had forgotten to invite him!

The Goose
That Laid the Golden Eggs

A man and his wife had the good fortune to own a goose which laid a golden egg every day. Lucky though they were, they soon began to think they were not getting rich fast enough, and, imagining the bird must be made of gold inside, they decided to kill it in order to get all of the precious metal at once. But when they cut it open, they found it was just like any other goose. There was no gold inside it at all. Thus, they neither got rich all at once, as they had hoped, nor did they enjoy any longer the daily addition to their wealth.

Much wants more and loses all.

This story is called "The Cat Knows Best." A farmer was very sad to find that his pet goose was dead. He said to his wife, "Look, it's that bad fox again. This time he didn't even need the goose for his dinner. He just killed it for sport and left it here. That wicked creature!" But his cat knew better. "It wasn't the fox who did it," she cried. But no one listened to the cat. Soon two policemen appeared. They looked all around and decided that the culprit was left-handed. And of course there is no such thing as a left-handed fox. So the cat was right and the

The Miser

A miser sold everything he had, and then melted down his hoard of gold into a single lump, which he buried secretly in a field. Every day he went to look at it, and would sometimes spend long hours gloating over his treasure. One of his servants noticed his frequent visits to the spot, and one day watched him and discovered his secret. Waiting his chance, the servant went one night and dug up the gold and stole it. The next day, the miser visited the place as usual and, finding his treasure gone, fell to tearing his hair and groaning over his loss. In this condition he was seen by one of his neighbors, who asked him what the trouble was. The miser told him of his misfortune, but the other replied, "Don't be so sad, my friend. Just put a plain brick into the pot and take a look at it every day. You won't be any worse off than before, for even when you had your gold it was of no earthly use to you."

Like talent, money unused has no value.

fox was declared innocent. The real culprit was never caught. But do you see him hiding underground, like a fox? The cat saw him there, too, but this time she didn't say anything. After all, no one had listened to her before. (Why do you suppose this man killed the goose? He did it because his child was sick and he wanted to give him some goose liver to make him strong again. He has the liver in a little bag and he is taking it home. Still, he shouldn't have killed the farmer's goose.)

The Two Dogs

The farmer had two dogs, one of which he trained as a hunting dog and the other as a lap dog. When the hunting dog had caught something to eat, he had to share it with the lap dog, but he did not think this was fair. "You don't do your share," he complained to the lap dog. "You just enjoy a good life while I work hard and get food for us both." "Complain to our master, not to me," replied the other. "It is what he has taught me to do."

Don't scold the lazy child, scold his parents.

A baby has just been born in this family, a little baby girl named Emily. Right now little Emily is sleeping inside the house. The celebration is just about to begin. The happy mother and father are getting everything ready for the party. The animals are all excited, too. They're going to sing at the party. The chorus will sound something like this: *"Bow-wow, moo-moo, ba-a ba-a, cock-a-doodle-do, oink—"* Oh, no, where's the pig? Maybe he's out in the back yard. The animals are whispering some-

The Farmer and His Animals

Once, during a cold and stormy winter, a farmer could not go out of his barnyard to get provisions for himself and his family. So he had to kill his sheep and cook them for food; then, as the storm still continued, he reluctantly killed some of his goats; next, as the weather showed no signs of improving, he was compelled to kill his pigs and eat them. When his dogs saw the various animals being killed and eaten in turn, they said to one another, "We had better get out of this place or we'll be the next to be eaten!"

Good weather makes a good master, but the weather can change.

thing to each other. It says, "They are worried that, with the baby here now, the people of the house might forget to take care of the animals or even to feed them." I don't think that would happen, really, but I suppose it could. It is true that when you were a baby, Freddy, you were the only thing your mother could think about. She said you were the apple of her eye. And our pet dog did feel a little left out.

The Shipwrecked Man and the Sea

A shipwrecked man cast up on the beach fell asleep after his struggle with the waves. When he woke up, he bitterly reproached the sea for enticing men with its smooth and smiling surface and then, when they were well embarked, turning in fury upon them and sending both ship and sailors to destruction. The sea arose and replied, "Do not blame me, O sailor, but the winds. By nature I am as calm and safe as the land. But the winds fall upon me with their gusts and gales and lash me into a fury that is not natural to me."

Don't judge a thing by its surface.

This is odd, Freddy (said Mr. Fox). It looks like an advertisement. It says, "The sun shines brightest after a storm." After that it says, "For a small sum you can buy your own security." It must be an ad for insurance. The boat was caught in a storm and sank. Naturally its owner was upset. But soon the sun came out. The owner hung up his clothes to

The North Wind and the Sun

A dispute arose between the north wind and the sun, each claiming that he was stronger than the other. At last they agreed to try their powers upon a traveler, to see which could strip him of his overcoat first. The north wind had the first try. Gathering up all his force for the attack, he came whirling furiously down upon the man and caught up his coat as though he would wrest it from him with a single effort. But the harder he blew, the more closely the man wrapped the coat around himself. Then came the turn of the sun. At first he beamed gently upon the traveler, who soon unbuttoned his coat. Then the sun shone forth in his full strength, and the man, before he had gone many more steps, was glad to throw his coat right off and complete his journey without it.

Persuasion is better than force.

dry, then sat down calmly and waited to be rescued. The point of the advertisement is that, since he was insured, even though his ship was wrecked he can get the money to buy another one. Maybe that's why they say that every cloud has a silver lining.

The Hurricane

A group of people set out on a voyage together. When they were far out at sea, they were overtaken by a hurricane which threatened to destroy them and their ship. Terrified, the passengers prayed to the gods, promising that if their lives were spared, they would make a special offering to them. But when the hurricane was over and the ocean was calm again, they soon forgot their prayers and promises and began feasting and dancing and rejoicing that they were all out of danger. But the captain of the ship, who was a very wise man, said to them, "It's all very well for you to enjoy yourselves now, but don't forget your promises and prayers, for another hurricane could come at any time."

Enjoy your good luck, but be prepared for bad luck, too.

Look, another storm! This time it's not an ad. There's a real storm over the ocean. See how the ship's rocking? It's worse than an earthquake. This is terrible! But maybe the ship is insured, so even if it sinks, the travelers will get their insurance money. Now, let's see, how many people are there on board? Hm-m. Ten people. That makes it easier to do the arithmetic. The question is, if they get one hundred dollars altogether, how much would each person get? That's one hundred divided by

The Enemies

Two men who were enemies were on a voyage in the same boat, so naturally each tried to separate himself as far as possible from the other. One man stayed at the front, or bow, of the boat, while the other remained at the back, or stern. Without warning, a great storm arose and the boat began to sink. "Which end of the boat will sink first?" asked the man at the stern. "The bow will go down first," replied the captain. "That's fine," said the man. "Then I can have the satisfaction of watching my enemy drown!" But of course his revenge was short, for his end of the boat sank soon afterward, and he too was drowned.

Do not rejoice in another's misfortune while you are both in the same boat.

ten. That's a good problem. Let's do it together some other day. But of course if these people sink with the ship, *they* surely won't get that insurance money. That's why they're all trying so hard to save themselves. What's that, Freddy? If they're saved then they won't get the insurance money either? Well, of course not. But who cares as long as they're saved? Life is more important than money, don't you agree?

The Blacksmith and His Dog

A blacksmith had a little dog, which used to sleep when his master was at work, but was very wide awake indeed when it was time for meals. One day his master became a little disgusted at this, and although he threw him a bone as usual, he complained, "When I am hammering away at my anvil you just curl up and go to sleep, but no sooner do I stop for a mouthful of food than you wake up and wag your tail and ask to be fed. But why should I feed a lazy dog like you?"

Those who refuse to work deserve to starve.

Hm-m (said Mr. Fox), there is one cat in the house on the left, and there are four mice in the house on the right. Ah-ha, I see. If the cat catches one mouse a day, in how many days will all the mice be gone? It's an arithmetic problem! But there is another story here, too. This man is a blacksmith. He makes iron horseshoes on his anvil, *clang-clang.* The woman next door is playing on her lyre, *strum-strum.* At first the black-smith's loud clanging just sounded like noise to her but after a while it

The Musician

A music student played on his harp inside his house, where the echoes made his playing sound wonderful, at least to his own ears. Because he listened only to himself, he soon began to think that he was a brilliant musician, and he insisted on giving a concert in a large theater. But when he did, it was clear that he couldn't play well at all, and the audience chased him right out of the hall.

A small talent in a small setting may look larger to its owner than it really is.

started to sound like music. And so she made up a song called "The Forest Blacksmith." Too bad we can't hear the music itself now but I'm sure you'll have a chance to hear it someday. A little mouse named Amadeus heard the song and thought it was beautiful. He made himself a harp out of strands of cobweb and played the song on it. His sister hated his music, but eventually he became a very popular mousician.

The Fortune Teller

A fortune teller set himself up in the marketplace and offered to foretell people's futures, for a fee, of course. Many people engaged his services. But suddenly someone came running up and told him that his house had been broken into by thieves, and that they had stolen everything they could lay hands on. The self-proclaimed prophet was up in a moment and rushed off, tearing his hair and calling down curses on the thieves. The bystanders laughed and one of them said, "Our wise friend professes to know what is going to happen to others, but it seems he's not clever enough to see what's happening to himself!"

Don't listen to false prophets.

Well, once upon a time there was a melon seller. He had lots of melons in his wagon, but here's a funny thing—they weren't real, they were all hand carved out of wood. Because of this, he painted a big picture of a hand on his wagon. A customer came to buy one of his melons. "Can't you make it cheaper?" he asked. "They are giving them away *free* at that fruit stand over there." Soon everyone began to shout, "Cheaper! Make them cheaper!" The melon seller was having a very hard time. Then, to make it worse, his wife came out of the wagon

The Astronomer

There was once an astronomer whose habit it was to go out at night and look at the stars. One night, as he was walking about outside the town gates, gazing up into the sky and not looking where he was going, he fell into a well. As he lay there groaning, someone passing by heard him. Coming to the edge of the well, he looked down and, on learning what had happened, said, "If it is really true that you were looking so hard at the sky that you didn't even see where your feet were carrying you along the ground, it seems to me that you deserve your bad luck."

Science without common sense can be dangerous.

and said, "Don't you *dare* make it any cheaper than it is, Pa!" Well, you might expect them to get into an argument about this, but what happened instead is that this customer slipped and fell into a well! ("Never play near a well," it says here, and that's good advice, Freddy.) Someone shouted, "We'll be right there to help you up." But do you see that bad fellow over there? He has taken advantage of all the commotion and is running off with someone's things. He is a thief.

The Hunter
and the Woodcutter

A hunter was searching in the forest for the tracks of a lion. Catching sight presently of a woodcutter who was felling a tree, he went up to him and asked him if he had noticed a lion's footprints anywhere about, or if he knew where his den was. The woodcutter answered, "Come with me if you are such a brave hunter, and I will show you the lion himself." At this, the hunter turned pale with fear and his teeth chattered as he replied, "Oh, I'm not looking for the lion, thanks, but only for his tracks."

Bravado is not the same as bravery.

Some men and a tame lion ran after the thief. The lion was known as something of a busybody, but he was trying to be helpful. The lion thought the man in the tree was the thief. But the thief was wearing a green hat, remember? And this man's hat is red, so he is not the thief, unless he is wearing a disguise. He claimed he was just looking for the thief, too. He said he climbed the tree so he could see a long way in all directions. "There's something suspicious-looking in that field over there,"

The Fox
and the Shepherd

A shepherd saw a lion chasing a deer, and hastily climbed a tree to be out of the lion's reach. The deer hid himself nearby, in the tall grass, and the lion came to the foot of the tree and asked the shepherd if he knew where the deer had hidden. The shepherd, not wishing the deer to think ill of him, said that he didn't know, but at the same time, he pointed to the deer's hiding place. As the lion leaped to catch the deer, the fox, who was watching the whole thing, said to the shepherd, "How untrustworthy and evil you are! You pretended with your words to betray the lion, but with your actions you betrayed the deer."

Actions speak louder than words.

he said, pointing. So the three men and the lion were all looking for the thief. But what's that you say? There's another lion there? And an antelope? You must be seeing things, Freddy. I see another animal, but it is a fox, not a lion. He doesn't takes sides, like the lion. That is, he just watches what's going on without saying anything. He understands both sides. But let's see what happens next.

The Bandit and the Mulberry Tree

A wicked bandit robbed and killed a man who was walking along the road, but the crime was soon discovered and he had to run for his life. A kind-hearted mulberry tree, seeing him running, said "Climb up into my branches and I will hide you." He climbed up into its branches, but he was found and captured, with his hands still covered with blood. Then the bandit said, "This isn't blood on my hands, it is the juice of this evil tree, which wants me to be blamed for the crime." But the people knew he was the murderer, and tied him to the tree and left him there to starve to death. "Mulberry tree, why don't you give me some berries to eat?" demanded the bandit. "If you don't, I will die, and it will be your fault." "I will not take pity on you," said the tree, "for you spoke evil of me and tried to blame me for the blood on your hands."

Even a very kind person may exact harsh retribution if his good reputation is attacked.

The people caught a man they thought was the thief and tied him to a mulberry tree. This man had a beard, though, and the man in town with the green hat didn't. However, that might also have been a disguise. The people who tied him up went to call the police. But they knew they would have to listen to what the man had to say for himself, too. They would have to believe that he was innocent until he was proven to be guilty. In other words, until the trial was over, they couldn't be sure if he

The Walnut Tree

A walnut tree which grew by the roadside bore every year a plentiful crop of nuts. Everyone who passed by pelted its branches with sticks and stones, in order to bring down the nuts, and the tree suffered severely. "It is not fair," it cried, "that the very persons who enjoy my fruit should thus reward me with insults and blows."

People are not always grateful—they sometimes return evil for good.

was really the thief or not. Compared with that, we foxes have a very hard time. Grown-up people think that all foxes are the same—all bad! That's why they'll chase a fox away even if it hasn't done anything wrong. But children are kinder. These children are gathering walnuts to give to the bandit. Then he might ask them to untie the rope. What would you do, Freddy? It does say here, though, that "the children should definitely not untie the rope."

The Woodcutter and the Noble Trees

A woodcutter went into the forest and begged the trees to give him a little piece of wood to make a handle for his ax. The biggest trees at once agreed to so modest a request and unhesitatingly gave him a young ash sapling, out of which he made the handle he needed. No sooner had he done so than he set to work cutting down the noblest trees in the wood. When they saw the use to which he was putting their gift, they cried, "Alas! Alas! We are ruined and we ourselves are to blame. The little compromise we agreed to has cost us dearly. Had we not sacrificed the rights of the ash tree, the smallest among us, we might ourselves have stood for ages."

The rights of the smallest must be defended, or even the strongest will eventually suffer.

This story is called "The Woodcutter's Dream." Once there was a woodcutter. He always worked very hard. He cut down trees and made all sorts of things out of the wood. He made a house, a table, chairs, a desk and a bed. The smaller bits of wood he used for firewood. His wife and child often brought him his lunch. One day the woodcutter surprised them by making his child a swing. But at first the child, instead of playing nicely on the swing, made a nuisance of himself. He pulled his father's hair and kept him awake. "Stop it! Your father

The Oak Tree and Jupiter

An oak tree complained to Jupiter, saying, "We oak trees are the strongest in the forest, but we are cut down more often than any of the other trees. Why do you make this happen to us?" But Jupiter replied, "It is just because you *are* the strongest that the woodcutters cut you down. The finest handles for plows and for axes are made of your wood, as also are the best houses and boats. It is because of your own nature that you are used in this way, and not because of the will of the gods."

There is no use complaining to God of misfortunes that come from ourselves.

is tired and needs a rest," said the mother. And she was right. The hard-working woodcutter was so tired that he fell asleep. But even in his sleep he kept worrying that he should go out and cut some more firewood so that his family would have enough to keep warm all the next winter. And what do you think happened then? Look back at the picture on the left. He began to *dream* that he was cutting wood. See, he has taken off his shirt again and is swinging his heavy ax! But now this is a dream. The woodcutter is chopping firewood in his dream.

Jupiter
and the Woodcutters

A woodcutter was felling a tree on the bank of a river when his ax, glancing off the trunk, flew out of his hands and fell into the water. As he stood by the water's edge lamenting his loss, Jupiter appeared and asked him the reason for his grief. On learning what had happened, out of pity for the woodcutter's distress, he dove into the river and, bringing up a golden ax, asked him if that was the one he had lost. The woodcutter replied that it was not. Jupiter dove a second time and, bringing up a silver ax, asked if that was his. "No, that is not mine either," said the woodcutter. Once more Jupiter dove into the river and brought up the missing ax. The woodcutter was overjoyed at recovering his property and thanked his benefactor warmly. The latter

There was once a magician who could do all sorts of marvelous things. One day he went to a pond in a forest where some woodcutters were at work. "Come one, come all! Come and see me change an ordinary steel ax to a gold one! There are no gimmicks! I'll do it before your very eyes," he called. "Here, lend me your ax," he said to one of the woodcutters. "I'll show you what I can do." The woodcutter gladly gave him his sharp steel ax, which the magician dropped into the water of the

was so pleased with his honesty that he made him a present of the other two axes. When the woodcutter told the story to his companions, one of these was filled with envy of his good fortune, and determined to try his luck for himself. So he went and began to fell a tree at the edge of the river, and presently contrived to let his ax drop into the water. Jupiter appeared as before and, on learning that his ax had fallen in, he dove in and brought up a golden ax, as he had done before. Without waiting to be asked whether it was his or not, the fellow cried, "That's mine! That's mine!" and stretched out his hand eagerly for the prize. But Jupiter was so disgusted by his dishonesty that he not only declined to give him the golden ax, but also refused to recover for him the one he had let fall into the stream.

Honesty is the best policy.

pond, cleverly exchanging it for a golden-colored one he had hidden there. He did this for several of the woodcutters, and they were delighted. But when they tried to use their golden axes to cut down some trees, they found they were too soft and dull to be useful at all. By this time the magician had disappeared and so had their good sharp steel axes. I hope their new axes were made of real gold, don't you?

The Mistress and Her Servants

A widow, thrifty and hard working, had two servants whom she kept pretty hard at work. They were not allowed to lie late abed in the mornings, but the old lady had them up and doing as soon as the rooster crowed. The servants hated having to get up at such an hour, especially in wintertime, and they thought that if it were not for the rooster waking up their mistress so horribly early they could sleep a bit later. So they chased the poor rooster and caught it and wrung its neck. But then they got a surprise. For their mistress, not having the rooster to tell her the time, woke them up earlier than ever, and set them to work in the middle of the night.

Tricksters may find they have only tricked themselves.

One morning the rooster said, "Goodbye, all! I'm leaving. I'm tired of having to get up so early just to wake up all you lazy creatures! And nobody appreciates my fine singing here, anyway. So I'm off to the city to sing in the opera!" Now there's a bird with spirit! You don't see that very often. It would go against a fox's principles to catch a rooster like this one. But the milkmaid and the cowherd tried to catch him. I hope he got away, don't you?

The Fat Hens

A farmer's widow had some very good hens, each of which laid several eggs each day. But she was not satisfied with this and decided to give them a lot more barley so they would lay more eggs. However, the hens got so fat that they could not lay even one egg a day, and so she had less than before.

Greed may lead to less, not more.

At the same time, in another part of the farmyard, everyone was feeding the hens. (But are these really hens? They're so fat! They are eating much too much.) "What can these people be thinking of, feeding them so much?" asked the water carrier. "We don't want these hens to run away," they explained. "We have made them so fat they can hardly move, so they surely can't run away." Well, Freddy, they won't be able to run away from a hungry fox, either.

The Cat and the Mice

There was once a house that was overrun with mice. A cat said to herself, "That's just the place for me!" Off she went to the house and caught the mice one by one and ate them. At last, the mice could stand it no longer and they made up their minds to take to their holes and stay there. "That's awkward," said the cat to herself. "The only thing to do is to coax them out by a trick." So she lay down and pretended to be dead. By and by a mouse peeped out and saw her. "Aha!" it cried, "you're very clever, madam, but you may turn yourself into a bag of meal lying there and yet you won't catch us coming near you."

Don't be deceived by the innocent airs of those you have once found to be dangerous.

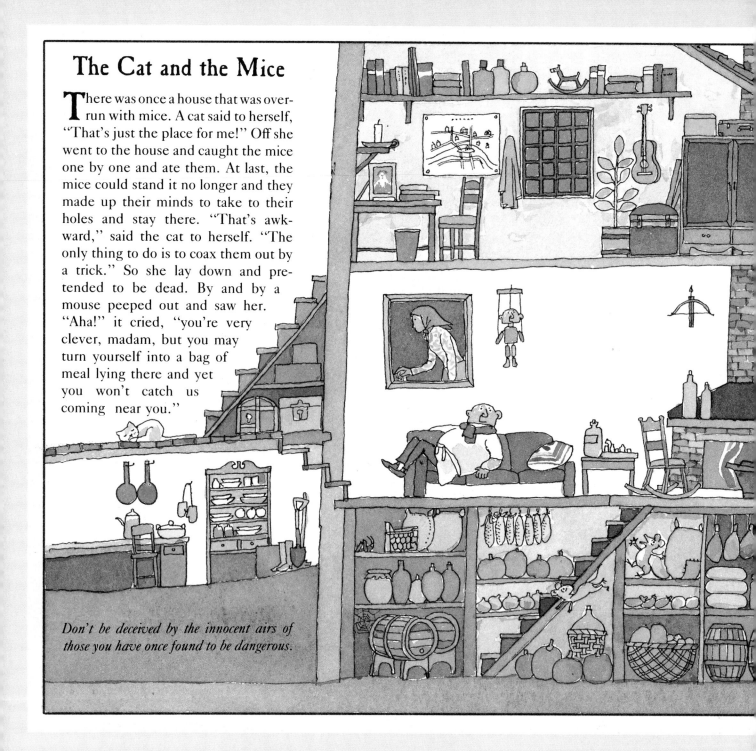

Look how big Emily has grown! She was just a baby a short time ago! Grandpa was taking a nap when he heard his granddaughter calling him. He got up at once. How happy he was to see her! "Hello, Grandpa dear," said Emily in a very sweet voice. Grandpa was so pleased. "Did you walk all the way here, Emily?" he asked. "Didn't you have your mother carry you? And how politely you greeted me!" Emily loves to

The House Mouse
and the Field Mouse

A house mouse and a field mouse were acquaintances, and the field mouse one day invited his friend to come and see him at his home in the meadow. The house mouse came and they sat down to a dinner of barleycorns and roots, the latter of which had a distinctly earthy flavor. The fare was not at all to the taste of the guest, and finally he exclaimed, "My poor, dear friend, you live here no better than the ants. Now you should just see how I live! My larder is a regular horn of plenty. You must come and stay in the house with me, and I promise you will live in luxury." So when he returned to his house, he took the field mouse with him, and showed him into a larder containing flour and corn and honey and all sorts of other delicacies. The field mouse had never seen anything like it, and sat down to enjoy the feast, but before they had well begun, the door of the larder opened and someone came in. The two mice scampered off and hid in a narrow and uncomfortable hole. Presently, when all was quiet, they ventured out again, but someone else came in and off they scuttled again. This was too much for the visitor. "Goodbye," said he. "I'm off. You live in the lap of luxury, I can see, but you are surrounded by dangers, whereas at home I can enjoy my simple dinner of roots and corn in peace."

Luxury may not be worth
the risks it entails.

have her grandfather read to her. The old man also likes to read to her. But his eyes are getting weak and he can't see very well, so he sometimes makes up a story or two. Emily is so good and polite that she always listens quietly and never complains. She's a lot like you, Freddy. You listen to my stories without complaining or correcting me. But then, it's not the same—Daddy doesn't make up stories, does he?

About Aesop's Fables

Aesop's fables are no more Aesop's than Grimms' fairy tales are the Grimms'. In both cases, the stories were probably of earlier origin and widely known, and were merely collected and popularized by those whose names have become associated with them. Aesop seems to have been a Phrygian slave who lived in Greece in the time of King Croesus. Although said to have been crippled or in some way deformed, he was extremely intelligent and a shrewd observer of human behaviour, and he was able to earn his freedom, eventually becoming a favourite adviser to the king himself. An excellent storyteller, he collected and retold a large number of "teaching tales," usually with animals portraying various traits of human character, through which he could point out the wisdom of good and just behaviour and warn of the misfortunes that would befall those who were evil or deceitful. His popularity at court combined with his outspoken and somewhat insolent manner, however, won him enemies as well as admirers, and he was put to death—hurled over a cliff—by the jealous people of Delphi.

Aesop's stories were collected and set down by various people. Chief among these ancient collections are those of Babrius, a hellenized Roman who set them down in Greek in the second half of the first century A.D. and of Phaedrus, who wrote in Latin at about the same time. In the fifteenth century a German scholar, Heinrich Steinhowel, made an extensive collection in the German language of the fables from these and various other sources. These were then translated into French in 1480 and into English soon thereafter, in 1483. Since then they have been told and retold countless times until they have become a part of the basic literature of all countries of the Western world as well as of Japan and other parts of the East. Their irony and perspicacity make Aesop's fables ideal subjects for Mitsumasa Anno to illustrate.

About Mitsumasa Anno and this book

Mitsumasa Anno is widely known for his imagination-stretching books for young readers. His books have been translated into many languages and are read and loved the world over. Their subjects include art and literature, nature, mathematics, philosophy, sociology, and history, but though the topics differ, a continuing theme underlies all his works. "Look, and look *again*!" he seems to say, encouraging readers to peer beneath the surfaces of things, to regard the world from a variety of viewpoints, to seek out the subtle but important truths that lie beneath confusing or deceptive appearances. In their own way, Aesop's fables, too, coax their hearers to probe more deeply into human nature and behaviour, and thus these stories lend themselves perfectly to Anno's artistic interpretation. But there are other possible interpretations of the illustrations, too, as Anno points out, and he wants young readers to think and decide for themselves what is going on in the pictures, just as Mr. Fox and Freddy do. Which version is correct? That is up to the reader to decide. Mitsumasa Anno says:

"It often happens that what we have seen with our own eyes, or what we have felt in our hearts is closer to the truth than the knowledge we have gained from reading words on a page. A thing may look differently when seen from a different angle. And so, I believe that even a child who cannot yet read words can still learn many valuable things by thinking creatively about what he or she sees in the pictures in this book, just as Freddy Fox does.

"Because I travel so much, people often assume that I speak many foreign languages. Actually, however, this is not the case. But, even if I cannot read the words that are written on the signs when I am in a strange land, I can usually guess their meanings and find my way. And so I get along quite well, although, of course, I hope some day to study foreign languages and to be able to read and speak them properly.

"But just suppose that I had a little son, and that I took him to a foreign country with me. Then I might *pretend* that I could really read the language, because I would not want him to lose respect for me. I certainly would want him to think, 'My father is a great man!' And if I made a mistake, I would try to gloss it over. Yes, as you can see, I am really a lot like Freddy's father, Mr. Fox!"

Mitsumasa Anno was born in Tsuwano, a historic town in western Japan. A graduate of the Yamaguchi Teacher Training College, he taught art in a primary school in Tokyo for several years before deciding to devote himself entirely to writing and illustrating. His works have earned him many awards and honours, including the 1984 Hans Christian Andersen Award, the highest honour in the field of children's literature and illustration. Mr. Anno lives in a suburb of Tokyo, but more often than not can be found in some other country, sketchbook and camera in hand, gathering material for another book.

REINHARDT BOOKS
in association with Viking

Distributed by the Penguin Group
27 Wrights Lane, London W8 5TZ, England
Viking Penguin Inc., 40 West 23rd Street, New York, New York 10010, USA
Penguin Books Australia Ltd, Ringwood, Victoria, Australia
Penguin Books Canada Ltd, 2801 John Street, Markham, Ontario, Canada L3R 1B4
Penguin Books (NZ) Ltd, 182-190 Wairau Road, Auckland 10, New Zealand

Penguin Books Ltd, Registered Offices: Harmondsworth, Middlesex, England

First published in Great Britain by Reinhardt Books 1990
First published in the USA by Orchard Books, New York 1989
First published in Japan under the title *Kitsune ga hirotta Isoppu monogatari*
by Iwanami Shoten Publishers, Tokyo 1987

1 3 5 7 9 10 8 6 4 2

Illustrations © 1987 by Mitsumasa Anno. Original Japanese text copyright
© 1987 by Mitsumasa Anno. English text copyright © 1989 by Orchard Books, New York.

Printed and bound in Italy by L.E.G.O. Vicenza

A CIP catalogue record for this book is available from the British Library
ISBN 1-871061-24-5

PUBLISHER'S NOTE

This English language edition of *Anno's Aesop* was first published in New York.
A number of sources were consulted for the text of the 'old' book discovered by
Freddy Fox, including *Aesop's Fables*, translated by V.S. Vernon Jones (London:
William Heinemann, 1912); *Fabulae Aesopicae collectae*, edited by Karl Halm
(Leipzig: Teubner, 1911) and *Esope Fables*, edited by Emile Chambry (Paris:
Societe d'Edition 'Les Belles Lettres', 1967). For some fables, however, Mitsumasa
Anno used earlier or more obscure sources and these have been translated
directly from his modern Japanese retelling. Mr Fox's stories are all original tales by
Mr Anno. The publishers would like to thank Michiyo Nakamoto, Hiroko
Watanabe and Satomi Ichikawa for their valuable assistance with the translation
from the Japanese.